World War II

Written by Sally Hewitt

W

FRANKLIN WATTS
LONDON·SYDNEY

First published in 2006 by Franklin Watts
338 Euston Road, London NW1 3BH

Franklin Watts Australia
Hachette Children's Books
Level 17/207 Kent Street, Sydney NSW 2000

Editor: Rachel Tonkin
Designers: Rachel Hamdi and Holly Mann
Picture researcher: Diana Morris
Craft projects: Anna-Marie D'Cruz
Map artwork: Stefan Chubluk

Picture credits:
Alamy: 17t, 17b; AP/Topham: 13t; Cody Images: 8b, 16;
Crown Copyright/Imperial War Museum: 10t;
HIP/Topham: 20b; Hulton Deutsch/Corbis: 8t. 22;
Picturepoint/Topham: front cover, 6, 9, 12, 13b, 20t, 24cr, 25t;
PRO/HIP/Topham: 24bl; RogerViollet/Topham: 7t, 25b;
Courtesy of Marilyn Tonkin: 26t.

With thanks to our model: Emel Augustin

Every attempt has been made to clear copyright.
Should there be any inadvertent omission please
apply to the publisher for rectification.

A CIP catalogue record for this book
is available from the British Library

ISBN: 978 0 7496 6504 3

Dewey Classification: 941.084

Printed in China

Franklin Watts is a division of Hachette Children's Books.

Contents

World War II

World War II was fought between 1939 and 1945. It is called a 'world' war because so many different countries took part in it. People's lives were completely changed by the war.

Invasion

World War II started when the German leader Adolf Hitler took his armies into Poland. He had already invaded other countries surrounding Germany. Britain and France were worried by Hitler. They warned him to move his **troops** out of Poland. Hitler did not take any notice.

Hitler led the **Nazi Party**. Here his supporters salute him at a **rally**.

On 3 September 1939, British Prime Minister Neville Chamberlain declared war on Germany.

World war

War spread from Europe across the world. In 1941, Germany invaded the **Soviet Union** and Japan attacked the United States navy at Pearl Harbour, in Hawaii.

The two sides fighting each other were known as the **Allied powers** and the **Axis powers**.

British Prime Minister Neville Chamberlain, 1937–1940. Winston Churchill took over from him in 1940.

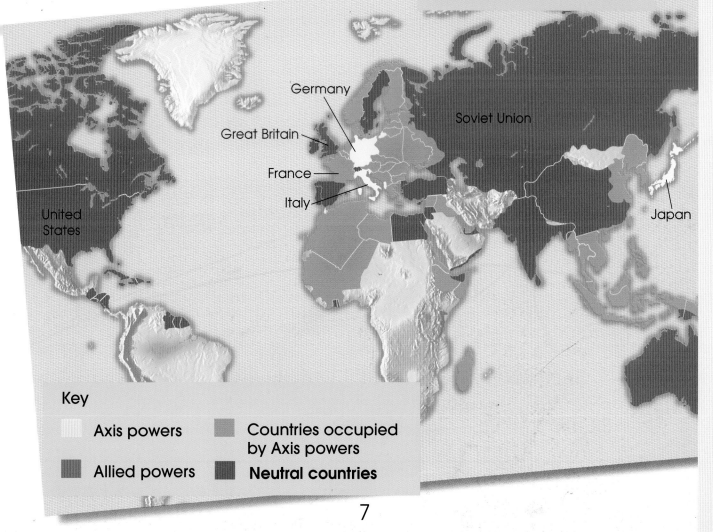

Germany

Great Britain

Soviet Union

France

Italy

United States

Japan

Key

Axis powers

Countries occupied by Axis powers

Allied powers

Neutral countries

The armed forces

In Britain, men joined the **armed forces** to fight against Hitler. They fought on land, at sea and in the air. Women without children joined up, too.

A father kissing his son goodbye as he goes off to fight.

Fathers did not know when they would see their families again. Women did not fight but did other important jobs instead.

Women joined ambulance crews and cared for wounded soldiers.

Soldiers, sailors and airmen wrote home. They had to be careful not to give away secrets, such as where they were, that could help the enemy. Children wrote to their fathers.

Dear Daddy

Imagine your father or uncle was away fighting in the war. You have just had a birthday. What would you want to tell him? What would he like to know? Try to sound cheerful and hopeful. Draw some pictures to illustrate your letter.

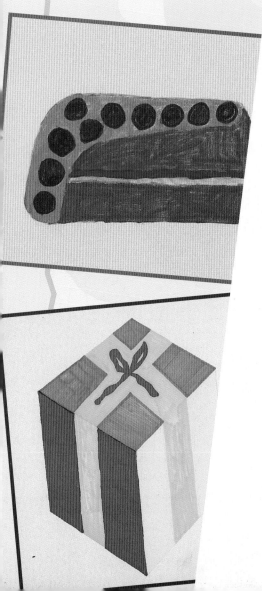

Dear Daddy,

How are y

Evacuation

The British government thought Hitler would invade Britain. They also expected bombs to be dropped on big cities.

Operation Pied Piper

The government decided to move children from the cities to the countryside, away from the dangerous areas. This movement was called **evacuation** and its code name was 'Operation Pied Piper'.

Many children stayed with strangers and some were very homesick. Others loved the countryside and even stayed there after the war.

Evacuees each wore a label, carried a bag of belongings and a **gas mask**.

Gas attack

Everyone was given a gas mask in case the Germans dropped poisonous gas on Britain. Masks for children were colourful and looked a bit like Mickey Mouse.

A boy wearing his Mickey Mouse gas mask.

Make a Mickey Mouse gas mask.

▶ **1** Copy the mask and nose shape below onto white card. Make sure the mask is big enough to cover your face. Cut out the shapes and the eye holes.

▶ **2** Cut along the dotted lines and glue the vent section to the back of the mask.

▶ **3** Stick the flap inside a 6cm cardboard tube, and glue on the nose. Paint the mask, copying the colours in the picture.

▶ **4** Punch holes at the sides and attach three strips of elastic.

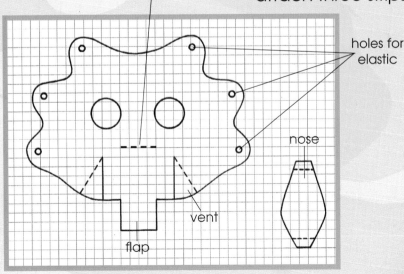

stick nose here

holes for elastic

nose

vent

flap

The Battle of Britain

Hitler planned to invade Britain. First, he sent the German Air Force, called the Luftwaffe, to attack airfields, ports and aircraft factories across Britain.

British Royal Air Force pilots flying Spitfires and Hurricanes fought the Battle of Britain against the Luftwaffe. The battle was in the air over the south of England from July to October 1940. Hitler put off his plans for **invasion** as too many German planes were shot down.

The Royal Air Force flew Spitfires, like these, and Hurricanes.

Make a model Spitfire

▶ **1** Cut out the shapes of the body, wings, tail and four propellers, as shown below. Cut along the dotted lines. Make your plane twice as big as the templates.

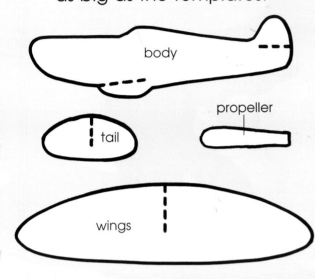

body

propeller

tail

wings

▶ **2** Paint the shapes in brown and green camouflage colours and add the **identification markings**.

▶ **3** Slot the different shapes together to make the plane

▶ **4** Make a nose out of Plasticine and put it onto the end of the plane. Paint the four propeller shapes. Stick these into the Plasticine.

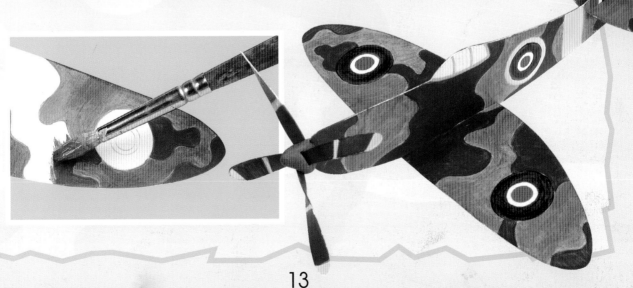

The Blitz

The Germans began to bomb Britain in September 1940. The main targets were big cities. This bombing attack was called the Blitz, short for Blitzkrieg which means 'lightning war' in German. During the Blitz, 41,000 ordinary people were killed.

Bomb damage to homes after an air raid in east London, 1940.

A couple preparing their Anderson shelter for an air raid.

Air raids

Lights from towns could help Germans see where to bomb. Street lights were turned off and people put up **blackout** curtains. During air raids, people went to shelters. Some shelters were in public places, others were in people's gardens.

Anderson Shelters

Anderson Shelters were made from corrugated steel sheets. A ditch was dug in the garden, then the shelter was put over it and covered with earth.

Make a model Anderson Shelter

▶ **1** Cut two rectangles out of corrugated card, 4cm wider than the width of a shoebox, as shown. Mark dotted lines the same width as the box, 5cm high and cut. Cut out a door on one piece.

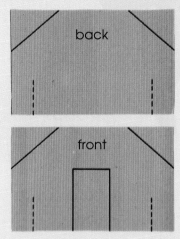

back

front

▶ **2** Cut out a large rectangle of corrugated card (about 40cm x 20cm). Bend and place it in the shoe box, as shown. Push it up to one end.

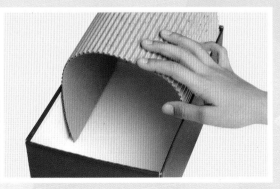

▶ **3** Slot on the front and back rectangles at each end. Put a piece of card across the front to make the ground outside and tape in place.

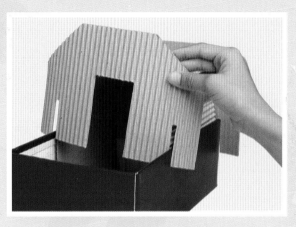

▶ **4** Now you have an easy to assemble shelter. You can add bunk beds inside or decorate the roof with a vegetable garden.

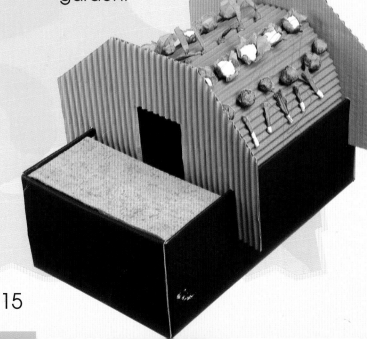

The home front

Those who couldn't join the armed forces fought on what was called 'the home front'. Everyone could do something, even children.

Men could serve in the Home Guard. The main job of the Home Guard was to protect the country if it was invaded. Unmarried women could work in factories and on farms.

Work for victory

The government urged everyone to do a few simple things towards victory. People were encouraged to grow vegetables and not waste food, clothes, water or useful materials.

The Home Guard protecting a train line from enemy aircraft.

Make a game – Victory!

▶ **1** Draw a grid with 49 squares on a square piece of strong card. Number the squares, leaving room for instructions.

1	2	3	4	5	6	7
14	13	12	11	10	9	8
15	16	17	18	19	20	21
28	27	26	25	24	23	22
29	30	31	32	33	34	35
42	41	40	39	38	37	36
43	44	45	46	47	48	49

▶ **2** Copy the game onto your card using bright colours. Decorate the board and cover it with clear, sticky-back plastic.

▶ **3** Now you can play the game. You will need a dice and some tokens, like coins. The rules are like Snakes and Ladders. The first to Victory square 49 is the winner.

Women in wartime

Women took on the work of the men who had gone to war.

They worked in factories. They joined the **Land Army** and worked on farms. Neighbours and grandmothers looked after children while their mothers worked.

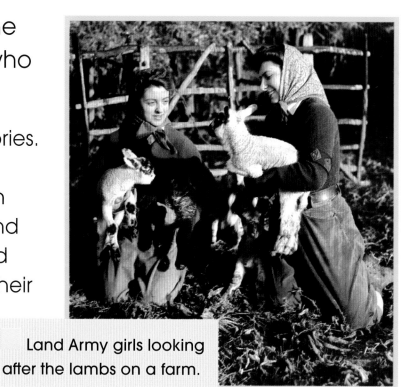

Land Army girls looking after the lambs on a farm.

In the Armed Forces

Single women without children joined the WAAF (Women's Auxiliary Air Force), the ATS (Auxiliary Territorial Service) and the WRENS (Women's Royal Naval Service). They did jobs such as driving ambulances and office work.

WREN air mechanics standing by a plane on an airbase.

Women also helped to break secret codes used by the enemy. Being able to read secret messages helped to win the war.

Write a coded message

There are many different ways of writing in code.

Here, a letter in the top line becomes the letter below it,

A B C D E F G H I J K L M N O P Q R S T U V W X Y Z

Z Y X W V U T S R Q P O N M L K J I H G F E D C B A

so **HELLO** becomes **SVOOL**.

WVZI WZW
R ZN RM GSV HSVOGVI.
DV XLFMGVW GVM KOZMVH !
Z YLNY OZMWVW EVIB MVZI.
R NRHH BLF.
OIEV YLYYB CCCC

Can you work out this message?
▶ Now write your own.

Answer:

DEAR DAD
I AM IN THE SHELTER.
WE COUNTED TEN PLANES!
A BOMB LANDED VERY NEAR.
I MISS YOU.
LOVE BOBBY XXXX

Rationing

During the war, food was scarce. The war made it difficult to bring in food from abroad so all food had to be produced in Britain.

Rationing

Rationing was introduced so that everyone got their fair share of food. Fish, fruit and vegetables were not rationed. Some people now had more food than they did before the war.

Everyone had a ration book with **coupons** to stop any unfairness.

Weekly rations per person
Butter 4oz (110g)
Sugar 12oz (350g)
Bacon and ham 4oz (110g)
1 shilling 10d (9p) worth of other meat

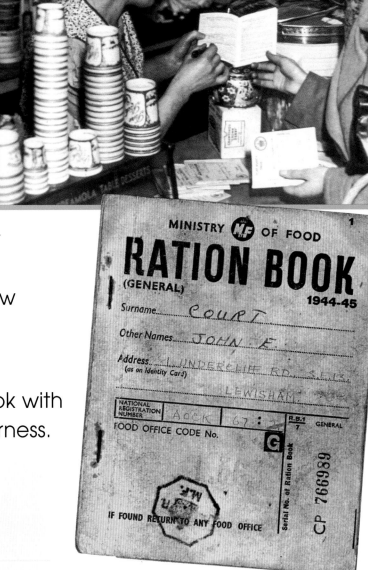

You handed in the coupons in your ration book when you bought food.

People were encouraged to eat potatoes. They were easy to grow, filling and cheap.

Ingredients

3oz (80g) fat • 8oz (220g) plain flour • pinch of salt • 2 tablespoons of baking powder • 4oz (110g) mashed and sieved potato • 4 oz (110g) cooked vegetables (broccoli and carrots)

Cook a wartime recipe
Potato pastry vegetable roll

▶ 1 Rub the fat into the flour. Add the salt and baking powder. Mix in the potato.

▶ 2 Add a little water to make a dry dough and knead well.

▶ 3 Roll out the dough on a floured board.

▶ 4 Spread cooked, chopped and seasoned vegetables such as broccoli and carrots onto the pastry leaving 2.5cm all round.

▶ 5 Roll up and seal the edges with water.

▶ 6 Brush milk over the top and bake at 180°C (Gas mark 6) for 35-45 minutes.

Make do and mend

Children had very few treats during the war, even at Christmas and on their birthdays. Materials and factories were needed for more important things than toys.

War toys

The few new toys that were made often had a war theme.

The pictures on jigsaws were of tanks, aircraft, warships and battles.

Knitted dolls wore army or navy uniforms.

Tanks and army trucks were popular toys during the war.

Toys were also handed down, painted and mended or made from unwanted bits and pieces.

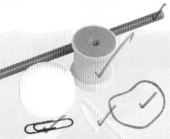

Make a roll-a long toy from odds and ends

▶ **1** Cut a length of straw to fit inside a cotton reel.

▶ **2** Take out the wax from a tea light and pull out the wick, leaving a hole.

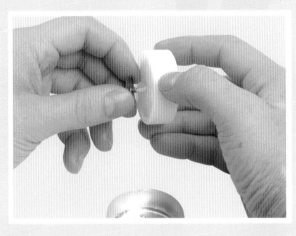

▶ **3** Ask an adult to cut the wax with a modelling clay knife so it is a smaller circle than the end of the cotton reel.

▶ **4** Make a groove across the top of the wax using a pencil point. This is for a match to sit in.

▶ **5** Make a hook from a paper clip and use it to thread the elastic band through the cotton reel.

▶ **6** Cut a matchstick in half, loop through the elastic band and tape to one end of the reel.

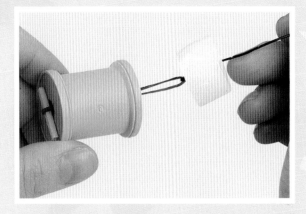

▶ **7** Thread the elastic band through the wax. Cut the tip off another matchstick and fit into the groove in the wax with one end overlapping.

▶ **8** Wind up the toy by turning the long matchstick round and round. Put it down and watch it roll along.

Poster campaign

The government had important messages they wanted to pass on to everyone. There was no television, only radio, cinemas and newspapers. Posters were put up everywhere telling people how they could help in 'the war effort'.

Serious messages

Some posters were funny but they all had a serious message.

The vegetable man encouraged people to eat vegetables.

DIG ON FOR VICTORY

A wartime poster encouraging people to grow their own food.

VEGETABLES for VICTORY Ambrose Heath

Everyone was encouraged to grow their own fruit and vegetables. These posters tell people that growing vegetables will help to win the war.

Make a wartime poster

The words on a poster were easy to remember, such as 'Dig on for Victory'. The pictures illustrated the message.

▶ Choose one of these wartime messages:

Don't waste it, save it

Keep cheerful

Don't use fuel that should be used for battle

▶ Make a rough sketch of your plan.

Make sure the picture can be seen and the words read from a distance. Use felt-tips, paints or crayons to create your poster.

Victory

In 1945, after nearly six years of war, Germany surrendered.

On 8th May, the allies celebrated victory in Europe. The King and Queen and the Prime Minister Winston Churchill waved from the balcony of Buckingham Palace.

Japan

War continued on against Japan. Then in August 1945, the United States dropped two **atom bombs** on Hiroshima and Nagasaki in Japan. These killed many thousands of people. On 14 August 1945, Japan surrendered and World War II came to an end.

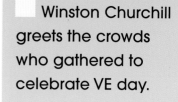

Winston Churchill greets the crowds who gathered to celebrate VE day.

The mushroom cloud from the atom bomb over the town of Hiroshima.

Celebrations

To celebrate VE day (Victory in Europe), people held street parties. Decorations were coloured in red, white and blue – the colours of the British flag.

People celebrated victory with street parties.

Make a victory hat

▶ **1** Cut a strip of white card 20cm high and wide enough to go around your head. Cut the top into a crown shape.

▶ **2** Decorate with red and blue felt-tip pens. Use the letter V for victory and the **Morse Code** for V ●●●–.

▶ **3** Tape the card to fit around your head.

27

Glossary

Allied powers

Britain and its Empire, USA, Canada, France, the Soviet Union and China. They fought against the Axis powers.

Armed forces

The armed forces are the army, navy and air force.

Atom bomb

The most powerful bomb of all time. It used nuclear energy to make the explosion.

Axis powers

The Axis powers were Germany, Italy, Japan, Bulgaria and Hungary. They fought against the allied powers.

Blackout

When lights were turned off or hidden at night so German bombers couldn't see cities and towns from the air.

Campaign

An organised plan to make something happen. A poster campaign made people aware of how they could help win the war.

Coupons

People were given ration books with coupons to make sure everyone had their fair share of food, clothing and other essentials.

Evacuation

Moving people out of dangerous places in World War II. Children were moved from cities to the countryside.

Gas mask

A mask given to everyone during the war to protect them if poisonous gas was dropped on Britain.

Identification markings

Special marks on planes so that other planes know whose side they belong to.

Invasion

When armed forces of one country march into or land in another country to take it over.

Land Army

The young women who worked on farms to take the place of the men who had gone to war.

Morse code

A code for sending messages by radio, using dots and dashes to represent letters and numbers.

Nazi party

The German National Socialist party started by Hitler.

Neutral coutries

Countries which did not take part in the war.

Rally

A large meeting to get people together for a special purpose.

Rationing

The sharing out of things such as food and clothing to make sure everyone gets a fair share.

Soviet Union

A former country in eastern Europe made up of Russia and 14 other countries.

Surrender

When one side in a war admits defeat and stops fighting.

Troops

Large groups of soldiers.

Index